THE MYSTERY OF THE LOST COLONY OF ROANOKE

HISTORY 5ᵀᴴ GRADE
CHILDREN'S HISTORY BOOKS

MW01258895

Speedy Publishing LLC

40 E. Main St. #1156

Newark, DE 19711

www.speedypublishing.com

Copyright 2017

In this book, we're going to talk about the mystery of the lost colony of Roanoke. So, let's get right to it!

When the English first came to the Americas, they settled numerous colonies. The very first colony they settled was on Roanoke Island. At that time, Roanoke was considered to be part of Virginia. However, once the states' boundaries were finalized, the location became part of the state of North Carolina.

Unfortunately, the colony failed and was eventually named the "Lost Colony." The mystery of what happened has never been solved.

NORTH CAROLINA MAP

QUEEN ELIZABETH I

THE LAND IS GRANTED

The British were in an expansion phase when the New World was discovered. They had territories all over the world and they wanted to add land in the Americas to their empire. Queen Elizabeth I granted land, which at that time belonged to the region of Virginia, to Sir Walter Raleigh in the year 1584.

Raleigh dispatched two captains to check out the area and determine a good location for the first colony. Captains Philip Amada and Arthur Barlowe found Roanoke Island off the coast. They met the Native Americans who already lived on the island. After surveying the area and getting a feel for the local people, they decided to recommend Roanoke as the place to begin building.

WALTER RALEIGH

RICHARD GREENVILLE

FIRST COLONY AT ROANOKE

Sir Richard Greenville was the leader of the first expedition to Roanoke. He and 107 men set foot on land at Roanoke in 1585. Once the men were settled in, Sir Richard left for England to obtain more supplies for the colony. He left Ralph Lane in charge in his absence.

The men had lots of plans for the settlement, but, from the very beginning, they were struggling. Battles between them and the Native Americans broke out frequently. There were other problems as well. They had arrived way too late in the year to begin planting crops to feed themselves. They hadn't prepared well and the supplies they had on hand were not enough to get them through the bitter winter season.

WINGINA

Their leader, Ralph Lane, was a military man and he thought his first priority was to establish a fort for their defense. The colonists built the fort and they built stone and wooden houses around it. The nearby Native Americans were seen as a constant threat. Lane was eventually responsible for having the Native American Roanoke chief, named Wingina, killed.

At one point, Sir Francis Drake was passing by the location on one of his many expeditions. The colonists pleaded with him to take them out of the location and back to England. Witnessing their struggles first hand, he agreed to take them back. The colonists got on Drake's ship and left. In those days, there was no means of communication over long distances, so they couldn't let Sir Richard know.

FRANCIS DRAKE

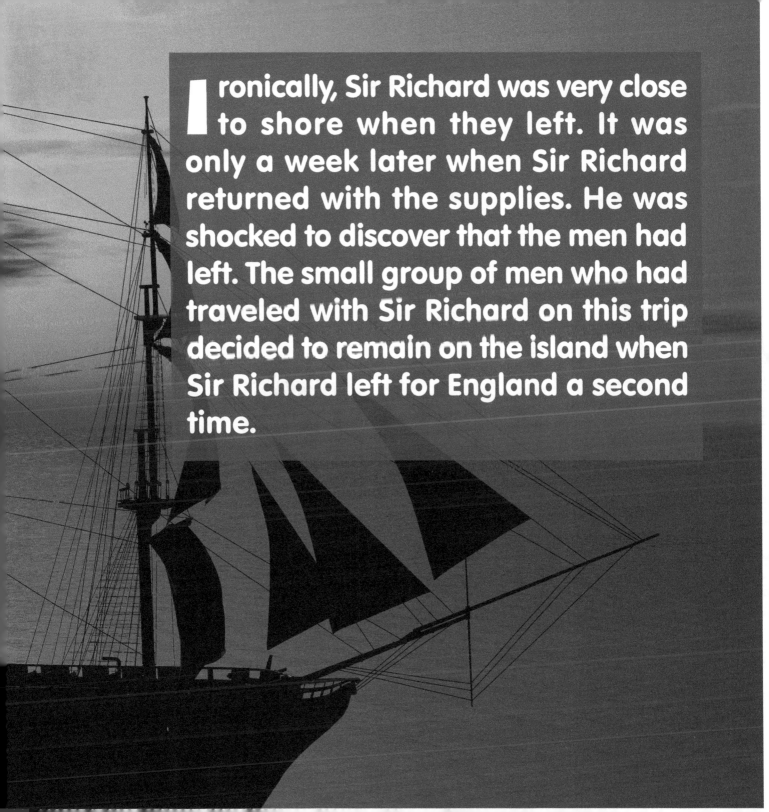

Ironically, Sir Richard was very close to shore when they left. It was only a week later when Sir Richard returned with the supplies. He was shocked to discover that the men had left. The small group of men who had traveled with Sir Richard on this trip decided to remain on the island when Sir Richard left for England a second time.

SECOND COLONY AT ROANOKE

Two years after the first colony, there was a second try at starting a colony at Roanoke. One hundred fifteen men and women traveled there and hoped to find the men that Sir Richard had left there the previous year.

A HUMAN SKULL IN THE SAND

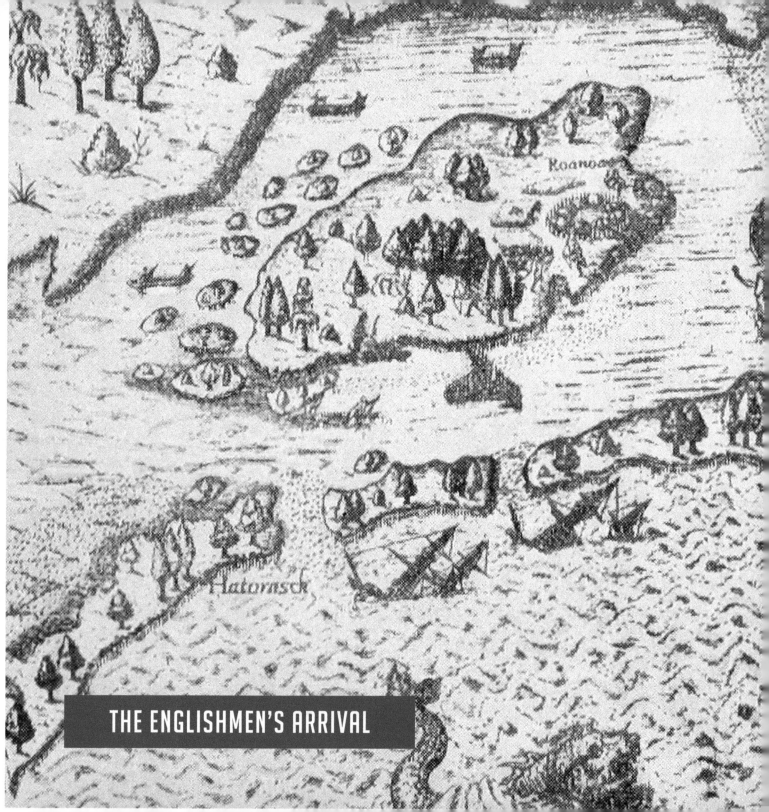

Roanoac

Hatorasck

THE ENGLISHMEN'S ARRIVAL

However, when they got there, the colony was abandoned. There was nothing there except the skeletal remains of one person.

Trinety harbor

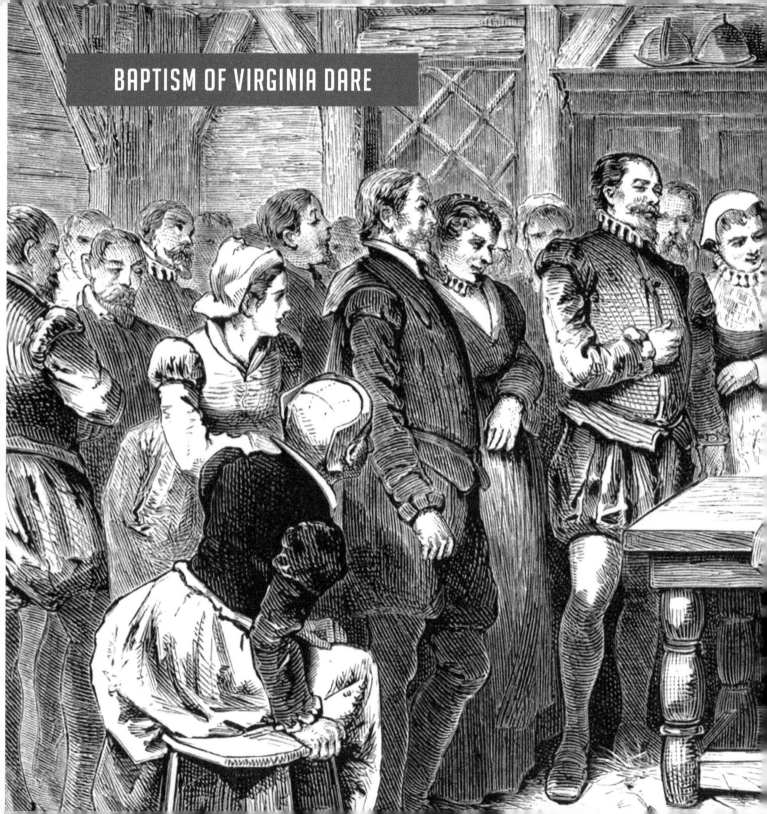

BAPTISM OF VIRGINIA DARE

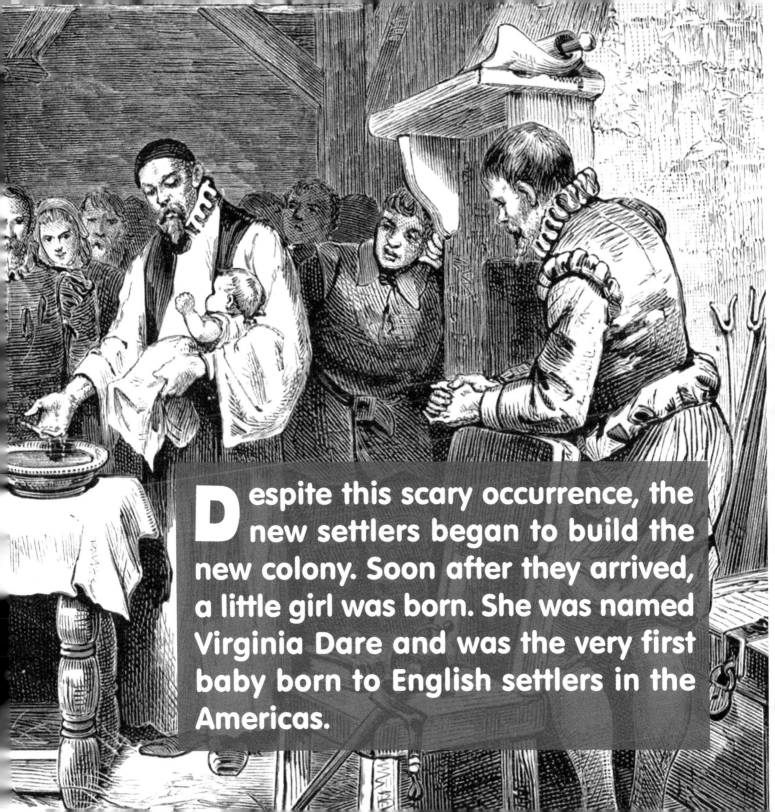

Despite this scary occurrence, the new settlers began to build the new colony. Soon after they arrived, a little girl was born. She was named Virginia Dare and was the very first baby born to English settlers in the Americas.

The ongoing battles with the local Native America tribes continued and led to casualties on both sides. The colonists weren't prepared for the hard work and struggles they were encountering at Roanoke. Their leader, John White, had to leave for the home country and bring supplies and more people back to the colony.

NATIVE AMERICAN TRIBE

SPANISH ARMADA

THE COLONISTS DISAPPEAR

Unfortunately, when John White returned to England, he couldn't get the help he needed for the colony. The reason was that England was battling with Spain at that time. They were engaged in a war with the Spanish Armada. It took White three years to gather the resources he needed and return to the island. When he finally got back, he was met with an eerie silence. No one was there.

White looked for clues to see if he could uncover what had happened. The settlers had not left any information for him. There were only two clues. The first clue was the word "Croatoan," which was carved into one of the posts of a wooden fence. The second clue was just "Cro" carved into the trunk of a tree.

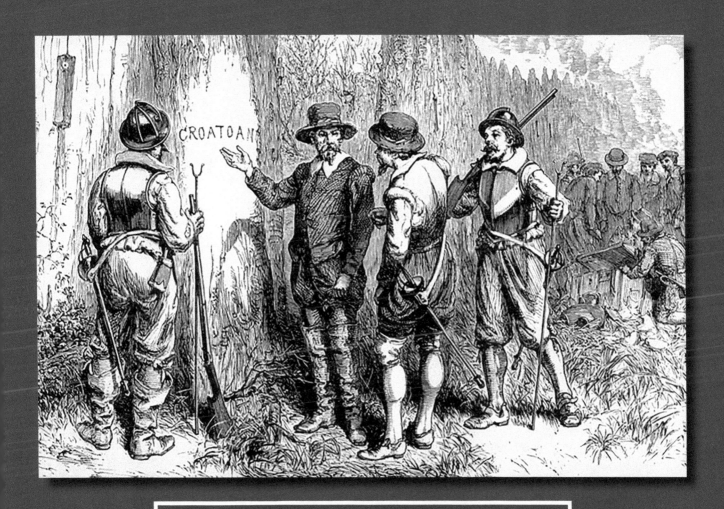

JOHN WHITE FOUND THE FIRST CLUE

THE MALTESE CROSS

There was no sign that any battles had taken place, at least not at the settlement. White thought that the colonists had moved to Hatteras Island, which was called Croatoan at the time. He had given them specific instructions to carve a symbol of a Maltese cross if for some reason the natives or other circumstances had forced them to leave the area. He looked everywhere, but no Maltese cross was found, so he assumed they had traveled safely.

He was going to set out for Croatoan, but a severe storm made it impossible for him to do so. Faced with being there alone, he had to return to England. No one ever saw the former settlers again. Forever after, their mysterious disappearance was noted in the history books as the "Lost Colony."

MOUNTAINS OF NORTH CAROLINA

THEORIES ON WHAT HAPPENED TO THE SETTLERS

There are many theories about the mysterious disappearance of the settlers. Some historians believe that it was the intention of the settlers to move to Croatoan. They may have made it there, but it's possible that stormy conditions or some other tragedy struck before they could settle on the other island. There is a possibility that they moved inland to the forests of what is now North Carolina.

It's also possible that they may have faced starvation or a disease may have swept through their population. The Native Americans may have rallied their forces and killed them.

A HUNGRY MAN HOLDING AN EMPTY BOWL

LUMBEE TRIBE

Some historians believe that they became part of a Native American tribe called the Lumbee tribe. Another possibility is that the Spanish, who were trying to colonize the Americas, came across their settlement and either killed the settlers or took them captive.

We may never know what happened to the Lost Colony at Roanoke, but some organizations are still trying to find out. The disappearance of the colonists emphasizes how difficult it was to start and maintain a settlement in the wilderness of North America.

THE CITTIE OF RALEGH

The 1587 settlers repaired the huts of the earlier colonists, built "newe cottages" and began life in the strange land. When their Governor, John White, returned in 1590, he found only the abandoned settlement with its log stockade. Located somewhere near the northern end of the island, the exact site has not been found.

ARCHAEOLOGIST WORKING IN FIELD

RECENT ARCHAEOLOGICAL DIGS

It's been over 400 years since the colonists disappeared, but recent archaeological digs are finding some clues about what may have happened to them. In 2015, a group of European objects including part of a sword, broken English bowls, and a piece of a slate tablet used for writing, which still had a letter inscribed on it, were found. These items were found about 50 miles southeast of what was believed to be their original location.

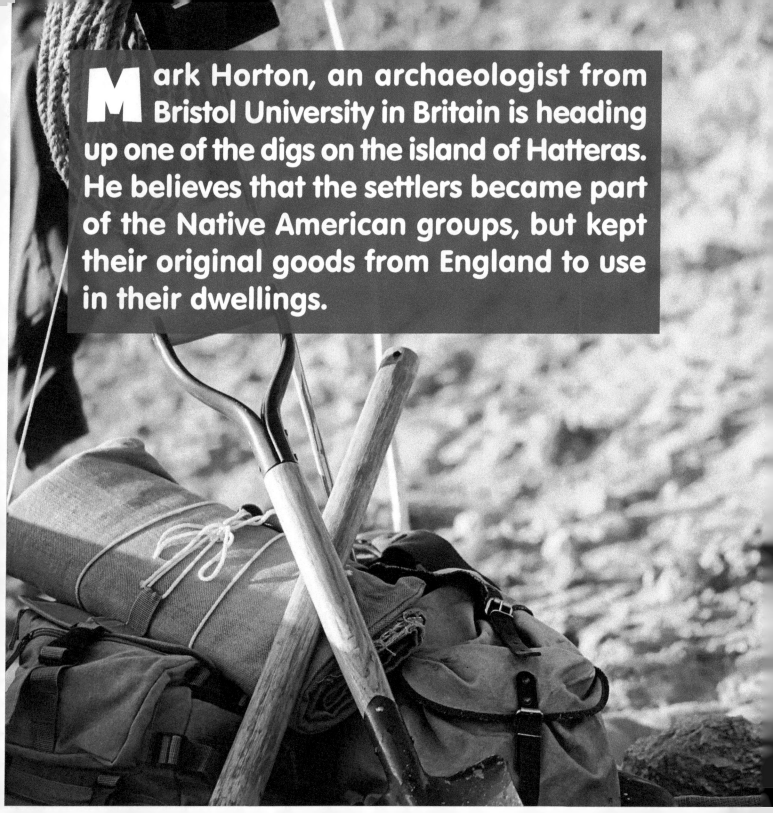

Mark Horton, an archaeologist from Bristol University in Britain is heading up one of the digs on the island of Hatteras. He believes that the settlers became part of the Native American groups, but kept their original goods from England to use in their dwellings.

ARCHAEOLOGIST IN TRAINING

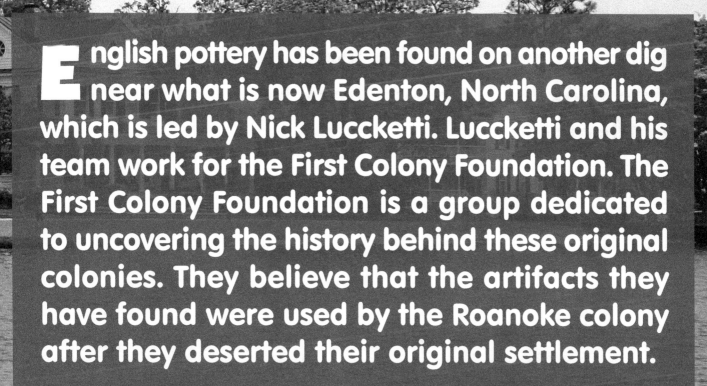

English pottery has been found on another dig near what is now Edenton, North Carolina, which is led by Nick Luccketti. Luccketti and his team work for the First Colony Foundation. The First Colony Foundation is a group dedicated to uncovering the history behind these original colonies. They believe that the artifacts they have found were used by the Roanoke colony after they deserted their original settlement.

Much more proof will need to be unearthed before it can be determined whether the colonists became part of the Native American tribes or whether the local tribes killed them and took their objects back to use in their own settlements.

NATIVE AMERICAN TRIBE

Scale

0   1   2   3   4 Miles

ATLANTIC

ROANOKE

Hotel

Old Inlet

Nag's Head

N.W.Pt.

Confed'rates surrendered here

Ft. Huger 12 Guns

Weirs Pt.

Ft. Blanchard 4 Guns

Armed Sch'r

Confed' Gun Boats

Dolby's Pt

Ballast Pt

Forrest 7 Guns

Redstone Pt.

3 Gun Battery

Shallowbag Bay

Piles and Sunken Vessels

Ft. Barlow 9 Guns

Pork Pt.

U.S. Gun Boats

ROANOKE

CROATAN

SOUND

Pond I.

House I.

3 Gun Battery

Fleetwood Pt.

Sand Pt.

Ashby's Harb'r Army Landed

ISLAND

Broad Cr.

BODIES I

MAIN LAND

Transports

Fishers

Bauens Cr.

Oyster Cr.

Broad Cr. Pt.

Marshes

Light Ho.

The Cut off

Duck I.

SOUND

FASCINATING FACTS ABOUT THE LOST COLONY

- **Virginia Dare was John White's granddaughter.**

- **The region of Roanoke Island where the colonists settled was only about 8 miles in length and a narrow 2 miles in width.**

- **In 2002, a bridge was constructed to the island. It was named after Virginia Dare.**

VIRGINIA DARE MEMORIAL BRIDGE

- Historians are not clear exactly where the colonists originally built their settlement. More than likely any remains of the settlement are underwater in the Atlantic Ocean.

- **Although Sir Walter Raleigh was granted the land in Virginia and orchestrated the colony settlement, he never set foot in North America.**

Now you know more about the lost colony of Roanoke. You can find more History books from Baby Professor by searching the website of your favorite book retailer.

Visit

BABY PROFESSOR
EDUCATION KIDS

www.BabyProfessorBooks.com

to download Free Baby Professor eBooks and view
our catalog of new and exciting Children's Books

CPSIA information can be obtained
at www.ICGtesting.com
Printed in the USA
LVHW060838130821
695227LV00010BA/179